My Mother Always Used to Say...

My Mother Always Used to Say...

ANNA TOCHTER

Angus & Robertson
An imprint of HarperCollins*Publishers*

DEDICATION

To my mother,
who always used to say . . .

'You'll understand when you
have children of your own'

Contents

Introduction

Like many women, it took having
children of my own (and a daughter
especially) to make me fully
appreciate my own mother and the
debt I owed her. Time and time again, my mother's
words come back to me as I hear myself saying, 'My
mother always used to say . . . ' Generations of
accumulated wisdom pass down the female line this
way, from mother to daughter. I have no doubt that
one day my daughter will carry on the tradition.

We are all the product of our mothers and their mothers before them. A funny mixture of values and prejudice, old-wives' tales and good old commonsense leaves its mark on the adult. To this day I cannot have my ears pierced or eat in the street.

Mothers were our guide in all things and knew everything, they were our first inspiration, they loved us and wanted us to grow up a credit to them. They set the rules and when reason failed they had the last, irrefutable word —

because I am your mother and I say so!

Anna Tochter

On Bringing Up Children

You give your children two things:
you give them roots and you give them wings

Nice Girls Don't . . .

MOTHERS ALWAYS ASSUME THAT THEY ARE BRINGING UP A
NICE GIRL AND THAT OTHER GIRLS ARE BAD INFLUENCES.
NICE GIRLS WERE ALWAYS IDENTIFIED BY A SERIES OF
THINGS THEY DIDN'T DO . . .

Get their ears pierced

❖

Wear black underwear

Eat in the street

❖

Smoke in public

❖

Swear or make a fool of themselves with drink

❖

Dye their hair

❖

Wear jewellery that makes a noise

❖

Wear shoes that need heeling

Bad Girls

Men don't marry girls like that

Other Mothers

I don't care what **other** mothers do!

Other People

OTHERWISE KNOWN AS 'BUT EVERYONE ELSE DOES IT' . . .

Just because everyone else is doing it,
doesn't make it right

❖

If everyone else was jumping off a cliff,
would you do it too?

Beauty Care

FROM THE FIRST ATTEMPTS AT MAKE-UP AND
WANTING TO LOCK THE BATHROOM DOOR,
MOTHERS WERE (UNFORTUNATELY) ALWAYS THERE
WITH HELPFUL ADVICE . . .

You don't need make-up at your age

❧

Never pluck your eyebrows

You make your own face

❖

If you pluck out one grey hair another seven
will grow in its place

❖

Brush your hair one hundred times before bed

❖

If you start shaving your legs now, you'll have to
deal with the bristles for the rest of your life

❖

One hour's sleep before midnight is worth two after

❖

If you don't keep your face out of the sun,
your skin will look like leather by the time you're 25

Acne and Other Agonies

It's just a phase

❖

Don't squeeze it

❖

Don't scratch it

❖

If you pick it, it'll never get better

❖

If you pick it, it'll leave a scar

Maternal Bias

You can't improve on a miracle

❖

Beauty is in the eye of the beholder

❖

Anyway, you have a lovely personality

❖

Looks aren't everything

❖

Beauty comes from within

Keeping Up Appearances

It doesn't matter about your clothes
provided you have good quality shoes

◆

Ill-fitting shoes show on your face

◆

Lift up your feet when you walk,
you don't want to wear out the ground

Clothes

You only need three of anything:
one on, one in the wash and one in the drawer

Precautions I

Always wear clean underwear in case you're
run over by a car and have to go to hospital

Precautions II

Always put paper on a strange toilet seat

Precautions III

Take a clean hankie

Precautions IV

Always carry enough money in your purse
for a phone call or a taxi home

Precautions V

Never do anything with a boy you'd be
ashamed for me to find out

Precautions VI

When in doubt — don't!

Mother Knows Best

MOTHERS HAD AN (OFTEN CONTRADICTORY) SAYING

FOR EVERYTHING AND ALL OCCASIONS . . .

Least said soonest mended

❖

Eavesdroppers never hear any good of themselves

❖

Better out than in

❖

Empty vessels make the most noise

If you can't be good be careful

❖

Don't care was made to care

❖

Out of sight, out of mind

❖

Don't make a fuss

❖

The devil makes work for idle hands

❖

Hear no evil, see no evil, speak no evil

Neither a borrower nor a lender be

Monkey see, monkey do

❖

Better safe than sorry

❖

There will be tears before bedtime

❖

Don't make mountains out of molehills

She's no better than she should be

❖

If you don't stop that you won't be able to help it

❖

More haste, less speed

❖

If a job's worth doing it's worth doing well

❖

A thing learned now is a habit for life

❖

Funny ha ha or funny peculiar?

❖

A secret's only a secret when you don't tell anyone

It's never too soon to learn

❖

Were you behind the barn door when
brains were being given out?

❖

Were you born in a tent?

❖

All things in moderation

❖

I've got eyes in the back of my head you know

❖

If you go to bed with wet hair,
you'll catch your death of cold

Manners Maketh Daughters . . .

OH, THE HOURS OF WORK THAT WENT IN HERE . . .

When someone asks you how you are, don't tell them!
Say 'Very well, thank you'

❖

Protect yourself from other people's bad manners
by a conspicuous display of your own good ones

❖

If you can't say something nice about someone
don't say anything at all

Manners are all we have to separate us from the animals

◆

Do unto others as you would have them do unto you

◆

Thank you letters must be written within the month

◆

Don't make personal remarks

◆

Don't point

◆

Don't whisper

◆

Children should be seen and not heard

◆

Speak when you are spoken to and not before

35
◆

Table Manners

IN BETWEEN THE ADMONISHMENTS WE MANAGED

TO GET SOMETHING TO EAT . . .

Elbows off the table, hands in laps

❖

Don't speak with your mouth full

❖

Don't read at the table

Flags were made for waving, not forks

❖

Don't start until your mother is served

❖

A lady never eats everything on her plate,
she leaves something for Miss Manners

Food

Crusts will make your hair curly

❖

Carrots will make you see in the dark

❖

Eat your greens or you'll get warts

❖

Eat your spinach and you'll get strong

❖

Chew it properly

❖

Don't play with your food

How do you know you don't like
it if you haven't tried it?

❖

There'll be no pudding till you've
eaten everything on your plate

❖

Waste not, want not

❖

Eat that up, don't you know there are
starving children in India who would love that?

Punishment

I'm only doing this for your own good

◆

You'll thank me later

◆

This is going to hurt me more than it's going to hurt you

Why?

. . . because it's good for you

❧

. . . because I say so

Sleep

Never disturb a sleeping child

❖

There never was a child so lovely
but her mother was glad to see her asleep

Can This Be Me?

There was a little girl
and she had a little curl
right in the middle of her forehead
and when she was good she was very, very good
and when she was bad she was horrid

Domestic Skills

MOTHERS ARE VERY SUPPORTIVE OF EFFORTS HERE,
NO MATTER HOW DISMAL. THEY CAN SHOW
GREAT SKILL AND DIPLOMACY WITH PHRASES
SUCH AS THESE WHICH PASS INTO FAMILY LORE . . .

It'll be better when it's pressed

No one will notice

You can only see it in the light

❖

Perhaps you could dye it

❖

A scarf would help

❖

Do you think that color is quite right?

❖

Here, let me do it

Objets Trouvés

Not lost but gone before

❖

If it were any closer it would bite you

❖

If I come there and find it, there'll be trouble

Education

You are being educated for a career, not a job

Emergencies

I told you to go before we left the house

Hot and Bothered

Horses sweat,

men perspire,

women merely glow

Selecting a Mate

Never trust someone who writes backwards

❖

Never trust someone whose eyes
are too close together

❖

Never trust a man who wears a brown suit

❖

Never trust a man with a dimple in his chin

❖

There are plenty more fish in the sea

Sex

It's just a moment's pleasure

❖

Boys only want one thing

❖

He'll never respect you in the morning

❖

It's the men who get the pleasure,
it's the girls who get the blame

Love

When bills come in the door,
love flies out the window

❖

Absence makes the heart grow fonder

Marriage

I married your father for better for worse,
but not for lunch

Marry a rich old man with a heart complaint

Watch the way a man eats; can you stand to see it
for the rest of your life?

❖

You've made your bed, now you can lie in it

❖

Marry for money and you will spend
the rest of your life earning it

❖

Marry in haste, repent at leisure

❖

What's yours is mine and what's mine's my own

On Not Quite Telling the Truth

Oh what a tangled web we weave

when first we practise to deceive

❧

If you lie you'll get a pimple on your tongue

On Being
Taken for Granted

This isn't a hotel, you know

❦

What did your last servant die of?

Gratitude

How sharper than a serpent's tooth it is
to have a thankless child

❖

After all I've done for you

❖

You'll thank me for this one day

Hygiene

Not to worry, we all have to eat a bit of dirt
before we die

❖

Don't put that in your mouth,
you don't know where it's been

On Learning by Example

Don't do as I do — do as I say

Making Faces

The wind will change and you'll stay like that

Mysteries I

Who did that? Mr Nobody?

Mysteries II

Men — neither use nor ornament

Mothers v. Daughters

Don't you give me that look, I invented it

❖

What's the matter, cat got your tongue?

❖

She is the cat's mother

Do you think I was born yesterday?

❖

They're not wrinkles, they're laughter lines

❖

After all the things I've done for you

❖

If I'd spoken to **my** mother like that . . .

❖

When I was your age . . .

❖

I'm not as green as I am cabbage looking

❖

Pardon me for living!

Arbitration

I don't care who started it — I'm finishing it!

❧

It takes two to start a quarrel, and both are wrong

Never let the sun go down on an argument

❖

Share and share alike

❖

Two wrongs don't make a right

❖

There'll be new rules in this house

❖

While you're under my roof you'll go by my rules

❖

How would you feel if someone did that to you?

Repeating Oneself

I've told you once so I won't tell you again

❖

If I've told you once I've told you a hundred times

Ways of Saying No

Maybe . . .

❖

We'll see . . .

❖

Ask your father

Retribution

God hears everything

❖

As ye sow so shall ye reap

❖

Wait till your father gets home

❖

Wait till I get you home

❖

I'll give you something to cry about in a minute

Economics

Do you think I'm made of money?

❖

Do you think money grows on trees?

Maternal Panacea

You'll feel better after a nice cup of tea

Eternity

A son is a son till he gets him a wife,
but a daughter's a daughter all her life

The Last Word

God could not be everywhere,
therefore he created mothers.

Jewish proverb

Angus&Robertson

An imprint of HarperCollins*Publishers,* Australia

First published in Australia in 1993
Reprinted in 1993 (twice), 1994, 1995 (twice), 1996, 1997
by HarperCollins*Publishers* Pty Limited
ACN 009 913 517
A member of the HarperCollins*Publishers* (Australia) Pty Limited Group

HarperCollins*Publishers*
25 Ryde Road, Pymble, Sydney, NSW 2073, Australia
31 View Road, Glenfield, Auckland 10, New Zealand
77-85 Fulham Palace Road, London W6 8JB, United Kingdom
Hazelton Lanes, 55 Avenue Road, Suite 2900, Toronto, Ontario M5R 3L2
and 1995 Markham Road, Scarborough, Ontario M1B 5M8, Canada
10 East 53rd Street, New York NY 10032, USA

ISBN 0 207 17849 6

Printed in Hong Kong by Printing Express on 120 gsm Woodfree

10 9 8   97 98